SIX NAILS
OF THE
CROSS

SIX NAILS OF THE CROSS

Sermons For Lent

BY WESLEY T. RUNK
AND THOMAS W. LENTZ

C.S.S. Publishing Co., Inc.
Lima, Ohio

SIX NAILS OF THE CROSS

Copyright © 1993 by
The C.S.S. Publishing Company, Inc.
Lima, Ohio

Scripture quotations are from the *New Revised Standard Version of the Bible,* copyright 1989 by the Division of Christian Education of the National Council of the Churches of Christ in the USA. Used by permission.

This book is a revision of *The Nails Of The Cross*, copyrighted 1971 by C.S.S. Publishing Company.

Library of Congress Cataloging-in-Publication Data

Runk, Wesley .
    Six nails of the cross : sermons for Lent / by Wesley T. Runk and Thomas W. Lentz.
        59 p.   14 by 21.5 cm.
    Rev. ed. of: The nails of the cross. c1971.
    ISBN 55673-560-X
    1. Lenten sermons. 2. Sermons, American. I. Lentz, Thomas W. II. Runk, Wesley T. Nails of the cross. III. Title.
VB4277.R86   1993
252'.62—dc20   92-37514
                                                            CIP

9308 / ISBN 1-55673-560-X
PRINTED IN U.S.A.

Over his head they put the charge against him, which read, "This is Jesus, the King of the Jews."

— Matthew 27:37

Table Of Contents

Introduction

The dramatic impact of this sermon series can be increased through a little advance preparation.

In previous situations where this sermon series was delivered, a cross was constructed to stand in the chancel area. Hanging from it was a contemporary form of a body, shaped from wire mesh. (The latter is not essential for the effectiveness of the sermons.)

Before entering the pulpit to deliver the sermon, the minister walked up to the cross and pounded in a nail, either on the upright or along the cross member.

These sermons deal with those ways in which we continue to divide and punish one another and the body of Christ through our sins. This visual and symbolic act by the minister prior to delivering the sermon made a deep and lasting impression upon the minds and hearts of many people.

THE NAIL
OF PRIDE

The Nail Of Pride

Ash Wednesday

As he taught, he said, "Beware of the scribes, who like to walk around in long robes, and to be greeted with respect in the marketplaces, and to have the best seats in the synagogues and places of honor at banquets! They devour widows' houses and for the sake of appearance say long prayers. They will receive the greater condemnation."

— Mark 12:38-40

One Sunday morning following the divine worship, the pastor greeted his parishioners at the door and accepted comments on his sermon. He had preached a searching sermon on the sin of pride. One particular woman had obviously hung back in order to confess her sin. When all the others had left, she told him that because of his sermon she realized what a sin she had committed during the past week. The minister asked her what the sin was. She replied, "My sin is pride. I sat in front of the mirror for one hour the day before yesterday and admired my beauty." "Oh," responded the pastor, "that isn't a sin of pride, that is the sin of imagination."

All of us realize that both conditions exist in the minds and lives of people. Jesus knew the paralyzing effect of pride and the terrible damage it could inflict upon the people's spirits. Of all the deadly sins, pride is perhaps the deadliest. When someone is filled with pride, he cannot experience spiritual growth. Some call pride "stiff kneed." A person with pride can never kneel to pray. Jesus had an image, a picture of what a person looked like, and how he acted when he was filled with pride.

In some ways it seems strange that Jesus zeroed in on the religious community with specific reference to the scribes. These were among Israel's finest. They were the epitome of a good example, and mothers cherished the hope that their sons would be like them. But Jesus said that men who despise manual labor, who court recognition with a passion, and who always expect the seat of honor at feast and worship while forcing the poor to their knees are a sad lot and filled with pride. These are the ones who pray loud and long. Such pride not only destroys, but also separates.

In Dickens' work, *Dombey and Son*, the effect of pride upon the human soul is described devastatingly. Dombey's whole life centered on his business until the birth of his son, Paul. The firm then became Dombey and Son and seemed to be more than compensation for the death of the mother in childbirth. But the father was not satisfied with normal progress and he drove his son toward excellence with such ferocity that the boy sickened and died. To overcome his grief, he married a beautiful and proud woman. When he tried to control her through means of humiliation, she humiliated him by running off with one of his clerks. Eventually the result of pride returns to where it all began with the failure of Dombey and Son. That night as he walked from room to room througoh his house with candle in hand, he came to the room where his son had slept and studied. He hurt, and he cried, but his pride was such still that if a man would have offered a hand, or a woman a tear of sympathy, he would have turned away in silence.

Our pride is not only self-destructive, but it is one of the nails that punctured the flesh of Jesus and held him to the cross. The torture and pain inflicted upon Jesus by our thinking we are better than we are is barbaric.

Jesus was stinging with his comments about the religious who survived on false pride. There were few who were not reached by his comparison of the Pharisee with the publican. "God be merciful to me, a sinner," is not only the insight of one man, but the key to salvation for us all. Any person who doesn't believe that he is in need of an overwhelming and undeserved love is unaware of his soul's trouble. The book of Proverbs declares to us that "Pride goes before destruction, and a haughty spirit before a fall. It is better to be a lowly spirit with the poor than to divide the spoil with the proud."

This day marks the beginning of Lent, the time when we concentrate upon our shortcomings, and the grace of God showed to us through the sacrificial death of the Christ. The key to Lent is penitence, a change of heart that allows God to work beneath the skin surface and rid us of our false egos.

Which of us cherishes the name hypocrite, or likes being the professionally religious? Not one of us. Yet with mallet or hammer in hand, we put the nail in place and ram it home with arrogance into the flesh of Christ.

Pride, such a large sin, takes such small steps. Pride in Sunday school and worship attendance, memorization of scriptures, election to boards of leadership, donations given to good causes, friendships with influential people, et cetera. What can we do so that we attend worship, read and learn our Bibles, serve in positions of trust, give generously and befriend all without sinning with pride?

We must always know the extent of our personal stature when it is compared with God Almighty. We must understand, too, that we do this all in response to God's love and his generosity to us. When we are serving, we know the true meaning of humility.

17

Tonight we see the placement of the first nail which hanged Christ on a cross. Its name is Pride, and it is deadly. Jesus died with one of these nails in his flesh, and we put it there. But hope always abounds for the penitent and humble, and this is the direction that the Spirit of God takes us.

Perhaps you would like to reappraise your life as you stand at the foot of the cross. Do you feel like you have a hammer in your hand, or do you weep in harmony with the humble who believe that he dies for all?

THE NAIL
OF INFIDELITY

The Nail Of Infidelity

Lent 1

While he was still speaking, Judas, one of the
twelve, arrived; with him was a large crowd with
swords and clubs, from the chief priests and the
elders of the people. Now the betrayer had given
them a sign, saying, "The one I will kiss is the man;
arrest him." At once he came up to Jesus and said,
"Greetings, Rabbi!" and kissed him. Jesus said to
him "Friend, do what you are here to do." Then
they came and laid hands on Jesus and arrested him.
Suddenly, one of those with Jesus put his hand on
his sword, drew it, and struck the slave of the high
priest, cutting off his ear. Then Jesus said to him,
"Put your sword back into its place; for all who take
the sword will perish by the sword. Do you think
that I cannot appeal to my Father, and he will at
once send me more than twelve legions of angels?
But how then would the scriptures be fulfilled, which

say it must happen in this way?" At that hour Jesus said to the crowds, "Have you come out with swords and clubs to arrest me as though I were a bandit? Day after day I sat in the temple teaching, and you did not arrest me. But all this has taken place, so that the scriptures of the prophets may be fulfilled." Then all the disciples deserted him and fled.

— Matthew 26:47-56

Friendship is an ancient virtue, highly valued among believers. The writer of Proverbs said, "A friend loves at all times, and a brother is born of adversity." The desire of everyone is to make each friend a brother or sister, and, while there is little hope of attaining this ideal, the failure to make an attempt is wastefulness and shame. To call someone our brother or sister is to put into words what our Lord desires in action. There is a story about the conversation held one day between the body and the shadow. The shadow was reminding the body how good a friend he was to go wherever the body went in sunshine or moonlight. But the body knew the true makeup of the shadow and reminded him of such when he said, "You are a friend in the sunshine and the moonlight but where are you when they do not shine and there is only darkness around me?"

The stories of David and Jonathon, Ruth and Naomi are glorious examples of the value which God places upon our human relationships. Jonathon was willing to face more than the wrath of an angry and jealous father, for he was willing to give up his inheritance as king and all of the power and prestige that went with being the first man of Israel. Friendship was never restricted to the unrelated. By law, in marriage men and women were expected to be friends as well, and to treat each other with respect and generosity. A common blood shared with other men and women, brothers and sisters, was and is an advantage to friendship and not an obstacle. Friendship — fidelity — is strongly desired by God and never overlooked in the teachings of humankind.

There are many true stories which tell the meaning of friendship better than any definition. The time will never come that the story of a daughter-in-law and her mother-in-law, both widowed, will not be related to a new generation. Separated they would have passed into oblivion, but together they became an example to all who needed courage when left alone in a world that seems a lot harder than it really is.

You won't find these names in the Bible, but in the 1960s you can be sure that Stokes and Twyman were words synonymous with friendship. Two men, professional basketball players, were good teammates and as such played well together. Returning home from an away game, Maurice Stokes was struck with a paralyzing disease. In a very short space of time this giant of a man had no control of his body or mind. No parent or relative, employer or lawyer, moved with such swiftness or desire as did Jack Twyman. At first he used his own personal resources, and then, when the situation demanded, he raised funds so that his friend could be rehabilitated to at least a partial form of what he once was. The fact that Maurice eventually died, or that he was black and Jack was white is irrelevant to the meaning of their friendship. Their relationship became the symbol for thousands of how to relate as friends as well as the goal for groups concerned with racial harmony.

Contrast this desire for brotherhood and true friendship with the horrifying situation of Judas' treason. Judas, disciple and confidant of Jesus, appeared at the garden of Gethsemane with the temple guard and some Roman soldiers to betray the one whom he said he loved with a kiss. No greater sign of love and affection can be given by one to another than a kiss, for it seals the very nature of two people into one intention. We are still shocked by the gall it took for Judas to finger Jesus out as the one the authorites were interested in through the use of a kiss. He didn't point, or lay his hand upon his shoulder or sit beside him. He kissed him, and in so doing designated Jesus as the one to be arrested and crucified. It was a despicable act. No reason, excuse or frustration seems adequate or justifiable to account for Judas' action. If it wasn't the 30 pieces of silver, then whatever the reason was, it wasn't good enough. His betrayal, this act of infidelity, was like driving a nail into the flesh of Jesus.

It wasn't that Jesus had never known or experienced hatred before. How well we remember all of the incidents of displeasure that he received from those who hated him. But Judas was a friend. He shared bread, shelter, moments of laughter and sorrow and the innermost thoughts of Jesus. Judas was not an enemy who wanted to savor victory in battle or triumph in debate. Judas was a companion to whom Jesus entrusted his earthly life.

Think of Jack Twyman refusing to use the money raised for Maurice Stokes' rehabilitation, and instead for his own personal gain. Make yourself imagine Jonathon leading his father Saul to David's hiding place. Picture if you possibly can a Ruth turning out her mother-in-law after her remarriage and you can gain a small measure of what Judas did to Jesus. The nail never entered Jesus with a clear and decisive stroke. The nail of infidelity split and crushed every morsel of flesh that it contacted. Judas betrayed Jesus with a kiss, a kiss.

We, too, are driving the nails of infidelity into the flesh of Christ with our own incomprehensible acts of betrayal. Whatever our reason, excuse or frustration, it is not good enough.

A man, respected by all, was asked to betray his trust with the promise of a better position, higher income and influential friends. The price was to give up his role as an active member and leader of a small congregation. It offended the boss' taste and his conscience and he demanded this this employee join his rank or the lines of the unemployed. When he measured the cost of his family, the years of hard work, the possibilities of the rewards, he accepted the offer and removed himself from the community of Christians. Most of what he was promised was delivered, but he regretted his act of betrayal far longer than the rewards lasted.

Every day we hear and see people willing to drive the nail into the flesh of Christ and we quietly acknowledge their behavior with sadness and disappointment. With regard to ourselves, we reduce the seriousness by calling our betrayal back yard gossip, ensuring our children's future, or just minding our own business.

All of the good examples of friendship will not make you any more loyal unless you are willing to take the chance that you will be used. Most people see their friendship as something of value. Like other precious things, they want to save it on a shelf for the right moment. Friendship is something to be used time and time again. It is your willingness to be used that makes your friendship so valuable. Once you have entrusted yourself to another there is no turning back.

Judas was a good disciple and a trusted one. There was never any question of his honesty for he was the treasurer of this chosen group. He must have had compassion for the poor. On one occasion he questioned the judgment of a believer who used an expensive perfume in the adoration of Jesus. This luxury, if sold, would have been a considerable amount as a gift to the poor. He said it, and one seemed to question his motive at the time or later. Save that one night or couple of days, Judas had an honorable ministry full of joy and service. But he broke that friendship with Jesus and with all others when he failed on that one occasion. His infidelity is so obvious that it can never be hidden.

What o₁ the others? The scriptures tell us that the other 11 fled. Some put up a temporary struggle for the life of Jesus and their own lives, but when they found out that they were not to t ʘ arrested, at least then, they ran. Peter even denied Jesus three times. They all broke the bond which had been established. Yet, in spite of it all, we see them differently. All 12 fell away from Jesus that night, but only Judas bears the burden of infidelity. The reason is obvious. The 11 came back. They asked and received forgiveness.

The nails in the flesh of Christ resulting from our sin of infidelity are permanent only when we allow them to be.

Christ forgives the sin of broken friendship just as he forgives all sins and all persons. Our reason for striking the nail tonight is not to do permanent damage or to enforce our individual sins of infidelity, but to impress upon us all the need to repent for wrong, and to receive the forgiveness of those whom we have sinned against, and ultimately the full forgiveness from God.

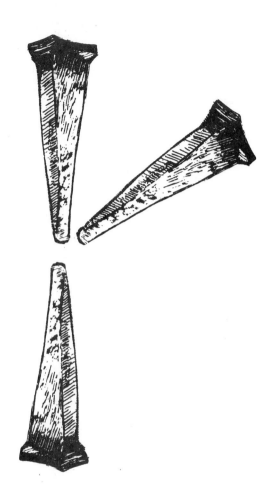

THE NAIL
OF ENVY

The Nail Of Envy

Lent 2

For he realized that it was out of jealousy that
they had handed him over.

— Matthew 27:18

When the grand hall was being built in Florence, the
committee in charge of decorations asked the most important
artist in all of Italy, Leonardo da Vinci, to submit some
drawings. There seemed to be little question that such an important hall should bear the mark of anyone but da Vinci,
but other artists also were asked to submit drawings. One of
the committee members had heard of a new and very young
artist by the name of Michelangelo, and asked him to enter
the competition. The sketches by Leonardo were magnificent,
but when the whole committee saw the work of Michelangelo,
they were so enthused that they gave him the job. When the
news of the committee's choice and the comments concerning

29

Michelangelo's work reached Leonardo, the old artist went into a decline from which he never recovered. Leonardo da Vinci spent the remaining years of his life in sorrow and deep envy of his young competitor.

The path of destruction left by the sin of envy is almost beyond belief. When we count the nails driven into the flesh of Christ, the nail of envy is found piercing the heart. The writer of the first gospel declares that Jesus stood trial because of the envy the priests and ruling classes felt for him. Their jealousy was so great that they actually desired the death of another man. It is hard to believe that one man would take the life of another man when the work done by the accused was good and for the benefit of all concerned.

There is a story told about an old saint who came upon two companions while traveling between cities. As they talked he noticed that one of the men was filled with greed, while the other felt only envy for the other. The saint told the men as they came to a fork in the road that he wanted to give them a gift before leaving them. He told both that he would grant one wish between the two of them and that whoever asked first would have his wish granted completely and the other would receive a double portion of the same. The greedy man knew what he wanted, but could not stand the thought of the other man receiving twice as much as he received. The man of envy also knew what he wanted, but he could not stand the other man getting what he wanted all to himself. Time passed without either of them saying a word until the old saint reminded them that he was going to take leave of them soon. Finally, the man of greed took the man of envy by the throat and demanded that he make his wish known or he would kill him. The man of envy agreed to do so and made his wish. "I wish to be made blind in one eye only," said the man of envy, and with that his wish was fulfilled. The greedy man received double the wish and was made blind in both eyes.

Envy breeds destruction, and all, including the envious, must suffer in the wake. Jesus died upon the cross and died a painful, humiliating death. But the envious were destroyed as well and suffered not only the inevitable defeat but also ever-lasting disgrace.

We look upon the death of Jesus as something which had to happen, part of a plan, and it was, but his death bore the sins of man and the result of our plunder. His death happened not because God thought it would be a good exercise for the spirit or to see if he could take it. Death was not a pleasant occurrence for God, but it was necessary to redeem his creation. In envy, to spite their own salvation, they gave Jesus up to the authorities and with imposters and false evidence they charged Jesus with crimes uncommitted.

Can you recall your last sin of envy? Do you remember when you tried to suffer in silence as another employee received some praise that you deserved? Doesn't it seem wrong for your sister to receive all of the attention from your parents? How about the neighbor who seems to always have some new piece of furniture when that person's spouse doesn't make as much as your spouse does? And this sin called envy isn't limited to the old or the mature. Not on your life! We recognize the real reason behind the green eyes when we see your ex-friend with the ex-boyfriend that you told to get lost. Isn't it envy that makes you so sure that the only reason the big kid is starting is because the coach is a good friend of his father's or is it because his father is running for school board? Envy, envy, envy, it will destroy us all, and, in the process, we are hammering that nail through the innocent body of Jesus.

Most of us are like Pilate, for we underestimate the capacity that envy has to destroy. Jesus was brought to trial out of envy, and Pilate thought that when the mob had a choice between an evil man like Barabbas and a good man like Jesus, they would choose to release Jesus. The choice was logical. Here they could have a murderer and anarchist roaming the streets, or they could have a religious fanatic who could heal and be kind to the poor. What kind of a choice would you and I make? The question should not even be asked. Of course we would choose Jesus and send Barabbas back to the dungeon.

But would we? This man who calls us hypocrites, and our leaders vipers? The one who ate with the unclean and broke all of the rules that we made holy and kept the community together? This is the one who got under the skin of our young people and made them reject all of the material things that we provide as passe while they look hopelessly for some utopia. These are the things that made the people shout, "Crucify Him, Crucify Him." It wasn't the idea that he would destroy the temple or that he would take the place of the Emperor Caesar. Envy, envy, envy.

In all of us this envy exists and its persistence drives us mad. Relentlessly we pound the nail into the flesh of Christ and make him die. We know that we are wrong, that our suspicions are false, but we need to save our face. How many times have you heard the remorseful comments that go something like this: "Maybe he was right this time but he challenges me so many times about things that he doesn't know anything about," or the daughter who cried, "Of course I don't believe that my parents love my sister any more than they love me, but then why do they come to visit so often when they know that my sister is the only one who has enough room to keep them?" And of course, the employee who sees his job as just doing what he is supposed to do and minding his own business feels envy but he really says to himself, "If he wants to make all kinds of suggestions and help the boss that's up to him."

We vote for Barabbas, but we really wanted Jesus to go free. We couldn't believe our ears that others were shouting for Barabbas, too. Then before we knew it the whole thing was too late. They simply took Jesus away and released that murderer into our midst. We need help. We need forgiveness. We need a new way of life. Get rid of the envy and do away with the nail.

Some years ago a man who was well known for his painting ability came to a museum and stood before some work of a known contemporary. For hours he stood and observed the painting with a critical eye. Most people expected him to be jealous and critical of what he saw, for after all, most people considered him to be second best and a few even credited him with being the first among contemporary painters. People stood about and waited for his comment as he stepped back from one of the masterpieces. When they looked at his face they saw a warm glow and then they read his lips as he said with a real sigh of humility, "And to think that they say I am a painter, too." That is the way God intended us to live with one another: giving recognition always to the other man as a person of great worth and not a rival to be destroyed.

Tonight as we leave, our prayer for each other is that we shall release the envy that has plagued us today and yesterday. We shall drop that hammer before we strike one more blow upon the nail and we shall ask for deliverance. No envy, just love. Never underestimate it. Pilate did, and look what it cost him. Give up the envy and rejoice in the well-being of others. It will make a new person out of you and it will have meant that Christ died to forgive what you have given up.

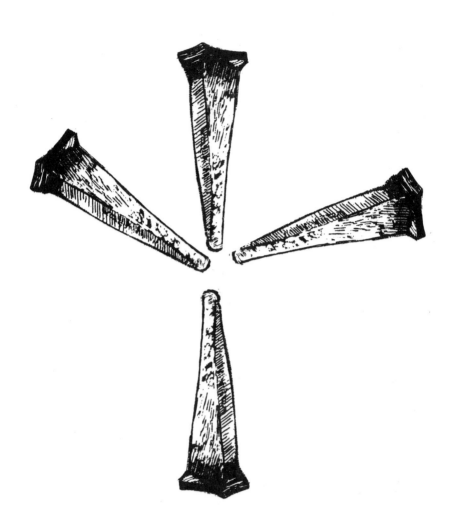

THE NAIL OF
INDECISION

The Nail Of Indecision

Lent 3

Now at the festival the governor was accustomed to release a prisoner for the crowd, anyone whom they wanted. At that time they had a notorious prisoner, called Jesus Barabbas. So after they had gathered, Pilate said to them, "Whom do you want me to release for you, Jesus Barabbas or Jesus who is called the Messiah?" For he realized that it was out of jealousy that they had handed him over. While he was sitting on the judgment seat, his wife sent word to him, "Have nothing to do with that innocent man, for today I have suffered a great deal because of a dream about him." Now the chief priests and the elders persuaded the crowds to ask for Barabbas and to have Jesus killed. The governor again said to them, "Which of the two do you want me to release for you?" And they said, "Barabbas." Pilate said to them, "Then what should I do with Jesus who is called the Messiah?'' All of them said, ''Let him be crucified!'' Then he asked, ''Why, what evil has he done?'' But they shouted all the more, ''Let him be crucified!''

So when Pilate saw that he could do nothing, but rather that a riot was beginning, he took some water and washed his hands before the crowd, saying, ''I am innocent of this man's blood; see to it yourselves.'' Then the people as a whole answered, ''His blood be on us and on our children!'' So he released Barabbas for them; and after flogging Jesus, he handed him over to be crucified.

— Matthew 27:15-26

Pilate was caught: he wanted to make the best of two worlds.

Should he sentence Jesus to death? That's hard to do to a man who has impressed you so favorably . . . with his innocence, with his strength, with his wisdom. But what should he do with the overwhelming opposition to Jesus? Should he, Pilate, take a stand against the majority who opposed him?

Releasing Jesus would mean an encounter with the Sanhedrin in the Jewish court, and Pilate did not want that. Sentencing Jesus would mean putting to death a man who had done nothing to deserve capital punishment. Yet there seemed to be only these two alternatives with their consequences: to defy the majority and the governing powers, or to defy his own conscience. But Pilate opted for a third alternative: to make no decision, to wash his hands of the matter, to repudiate his responsibility.

If Christianity has anything to say in the area of ethics and morality, one thing is certain: it does not recognize morally neutral situations. The ethic of Christianity is either/or. There is no third way beside doing good or evil. To do nothing is equivalent to doing evil. As it is written in Revelation: ''I know your works; you are neither cold nor hot. Would that you were cold or hot. So, because you are lukewarm, and neither cold nor hot, I will spew you out of my mouth." Or listen to the prophet whose words leave no room for moral ambiguity. "Choose the good that you might live. Hate the evil and love the good." On the words of Joshua, "And if you be unwilling to serve the Lord, choose this day whom you will serve . . ."

Our Lord's own command issues forth the same call for unequivocal obedience. "You shall love the Lord your God with all your heart, soul, mind and strength." The call of discipleship is black and white. It is an either/or situation. When Jesus called his disciples he made it quite plain that there was no room for compromise: he said, follow me, even if it means to turn your back on mother or father. To the young man who wanted to bury his dead relative first, Jesus said, "No, leave the dead to bury the dead." He left no room for procrastination, for excuses.

In the gospels, the way of the cross appears difficult; it involves suffering and trial, but the choice is still black and white. In both the Old and New Testaments, the issues of life are seen in terms of faithfulness. The Christian life is pictured as doing battle in the world, and this battle belongs not to the strong, or the wise, but to the faithful. Paul's letter to the Ephesians exhorts Christians to put on the whole armor of God. One must be faithful and strong to stand. The Psalmist speaks of double-minded men who are rebuked by God. But the promise to those who make a single-minded decision is God's peace which passes all understanding.

To live is to choose. It is the very negation of life to act against one's better judgment through weakness, because one doesn't dare to take the responsibility for one's decisions. Prolonged indecision is a poison in one's life. It indicates a prolonged fear to face responsibility. To make a decision is to be willing to accept the responsibility for what one chooses.

Domineering parents may thwart the decision-making process in a child in a way which may persist throughout his life, not by the strictness of their discipline, but by making all the child's decisions for him. When that child becomes an adult, he does not know what his tastes are, his beliefs, his aim in life. As soon as this person does make a decision, he begins to wonder if he had not made a mistake. And so he is content to let others make decisions for him. His constant concern is to shelter himself under the authority of others.

When persons such as this come to us seeking advice, we have an obligation not to make their decisions for them, but to help them make their own decisions.

When parents or friends decide everything for a child or adult, it indicates that they do not trust his judgment. Thus, they have sown in him a lack of self-confidence, which makes him weak, incapable of decision, less than adult. And so trust is of prime importance — trust in the person's ability to make a responsible choice, even if the decision seems questionable to us sometimes.

I read recently that worry is created by those who live in the past or the future, but never in the present. These people live provisional lives, their lives are never in their present lives for they are always waiting for the time, which never comes, when their true lives will begin.

Some women merely tolerate their lives. Each day, while their children are young, they wait for those moments of liberation when their children are grown and they can at last do the things they want. These are the very ones who find themselves at a loss, unprepared to enjoy those moments of freedom when they do come; for they have not learned to live in the present.

The same thing is true in the case of persons who look upon their present occupations as provisional. In such a state of mind they lose all interest and pleasure in their work. Perhaps they go frequently from one provisional employment to another and their ability to throw themselves heart and soul into their work diminishes daily.

Many do not even realize that what determined their occupation was a set of circumstances in the face of which they remained entirely passive, so that on their part there was nothing that could be called a choice.

Having a vocation means acting in the spirit of vocation, being convinced that what one is doing is what one is called to do. And if a person should realize that his occupation does not fit in with his ambitions, it means risking the choice of change. Sometimes the rebirth of a person takes place when such a risk is ventured, even at the cost of material security.

But let us not fall into the trap of thinking that it matters little what choice or decision we make, so long as we do choose or decide. This would be like the young girl who said we must experience all things for ourselves. To choose to experience all things is to ignore that all experiences are not equally good. A true choice necessarily implies reference to a scale of values. The Bible is indeed the book which demands decisions but not blind decisions. For it shows us where true life and liberty are to be found.

One of the problems which plagues youth today is not that they do not choose, but that they do not carry their choice far enough. True, there is hypocrisy and materialism in our culture, and the social drop-outs may have a legitimate complaint when they regard our culture as a sham. But their lives contain no vision, no hope, for they are shaped and molded around rebellion, revolt. The child may choose to reject the authority of his parents. But he must realize that this is not enough. That will not nourish his life. He must choose another truly personal inspiration. He is oppressed by his parents' domination. To prove himself no longer a child, he defies it. It is a movement toward liberty, but it is not liberty itself. Decisions are not true decisions if they are merely in reaction or rebellion to the status quo. The world is full of too many of those who merely decide by taking the opposing viewpoint, with no other rational reasons, than taking pride in belonging to the opposition. These peoples' lives are not their own, for they are not determined by their own goals and visions.

But how do we escape the nail of indecision in our lives today? What can we do?

First of all, most issues today come to us crystal clearly; it is not a matter of what to do, but will I in fact do what

I know in my heart is right? Most of the issues of life are clear: I know that I should seek out the lonely, rather than only my friends all the time; I know that I should forgive my neighbor instead of maintaining my hostility toward him; I know that I should give up my party strife. In many of these things no amount of preaching or church-going can turn the will of a person until he decides for himself that the decision of obedience has to be made if he is to find peace of mind.

Yet in other issues confusion remains. Sometimes the ethical problems today are not merely a matter of obedience or disobedience. Sometimes the evidence seems to weigh equally on either side. While our commitment to God is black or white, either/or, it can't be totally identified with our commitments in the world. The context of the world is one of compromise. Equally Christians can take opposing sides on many political issues.

And so we have to determine what areas in our lives can be decided entirely by disobedience or obedience, and those areas which require more information, more questioning, a different strategy.

Some say, inflation or not, you can still get a decision from a tossed nickel.

But that is not the way to responsible decisions. In these areas, we must collect the evidence, we must be responsible citizens, and then in the milieu of a sinful world, we must make the best decision we can. But we must always realize that our worldly decisions can not contain the ultimate solution. There is no person, no clerical body, no ethical principle that always works. There is no group of people who have all the answers.

And this is the reason we meet in a body; we learn to await the Spirit; to listen with open heart and mind to the scripture, to learn the will of God. The church under pressure waits for God, and it maintains an openness to the living spirit of the eternal God.

THE NAIL
OF HATRED

The Nail Of Hatred

Lent 4

"Blessed are you when people hate you, and when they exclude you, revile you, and defame you on account of the Son of Man."

"If you love those who love you, what credit is that to you? For even sinners love those who love them. If you do good to those who do good to you, what credit is that to you? For even sinners do the same. If you lend to those from whom you hope to receive, what credit is that to you? Even sinners lend to sinners, to receive as much again. But love your enemies, do good, and lend, expecting nothing in return. Your reward will be great, and you will be children of the Most High; for he is kind to the ungrateful and the wicked.

— Luke 6:22, 32-35

Hatred rings out in the world like the shrill clash of metal against metal; the hammer against the nail.

Hatred is the force of darkness that covers the face of the earth, reaping destruction where it goes.

Hatred is most often aroused by our self-righteous resentments. It is easier to shoot the villains, to seek retribution for the satisfaction of our moral feelings, than to get at the root of villainy or to transform the villain. It is easier to kill bad people than to build bridges.

The passion hatred, which periodically sweeps through people like a storm is almost always misdirected. It is easier to kill the villain than to build bridges of trust and understanding.

Ethnic mistrust breeds and thrives on hatred. It is hatred that breeds apartheid, anti-semitism and other forms of ethnic mistrust. Hatred causes strife in places like Yugoslavia, Palestine, South Africa and Los Angeles.

The actions of that hatred often create poverty, sin and human misery. What a difference it would make if our hatreds were redirected.

"Hate the evil, love the good, and you will establish justice," said Amos.

Hatred does not begin on such a full-scale level. It begins within each one of us. When our rights, our goals, our interests, our jobs are threatened — these things which are so central to our identity, our purpose, our being — it is then that we strike out in fear and hatred.

Bishop Nygren once put it this way in a commencement address at Carthage College:

> *Let us imagine that we are walking on a large plain. We can see in all directions. If I look around, I see the line of the horizon like a line of a circle. Where does this circle have its center? Answer: Just where I happen to stand! Wherever I view the world I always stand quite naturally in the center. Wherever I go, I take the center with me. Wherever I am, I have always the zenith above me. All the lines from the horizon converge in the individual "I" at the center.*

It belongs to the nature of the "I" to occupy a central position. Theoretically viewed this creates very little difficulty. Even if I see everything from my own point of view, even if it appears to be so for me, as if I were the center of the universe — still I know that I am not the center of the universe, but just a small speck of the universe, chosen at random. I know how it is, and so this illusion does not have any serious consequences.

Great complications, however, develop within the sphere of the will and of human action. Here, too, there exists the same centralization around the individual "I." I see it clearly: it is my interest, my private business that is in the center. The interests of my fellow men are more or less on the outskirts. This is how man thinks of himself. And when there is a conflict between different interests, the fight begins: the fight between individuals, the fight between different social classes, the fight between the races, the fight between nations, the fight between East and West.

It must be so in a world without a real center, where everybody walks about having the center in himself.

Hatred grows out of a limitation which is forced upon us by having to live with one another and it reaches out to destroy that limiting presence. Hatred is the force and power of destruction. It leads away from life to death.

Psychologists tell us that the emotion of hatred produces more immediate effects on the chemical balance of the body than any other emotion, including fear, and that while the emotion itself may pass swiftly, the damage doesn't. "It's all over in a minute," we say. So is a cyclone . . . but then the wreckage has to be cleaned up.

Hatred is also the cry from one who has not fully realized the purpose of his life. Like the baby who screams in rage, "Somebody took my rattle," men and women scream in blind rage, "Somebody stole my glory, somebody ruined my life, or the best years of it, somebody infringed upon my rights."

They say you can tell the size of a person by the size of the thing that makes the person mad. They also say that persons wrapped up in themselves make a small package. How often are anger, hatred, wrath aroused over this small package.

The world loves to tell us that what is most important is what makes "me" most important. The world loves to tell us that value is measured by the strength of my voice, the size of the group which will come and hear it; the world loves to tell us that value is determined by success, not lowliness. Success is the ability to stand while others fall, the ability to climb over and above the others.

Christ came preaching a different message. "Deny yourselves," he said. In humility count others better than yourselves. Look not merely to your own interest, but to the interests of others. Be even like me . . . who came not among you to display power and glory, but to empty myself, to take the form of a servant.

Does the world like this standard? No, it loves only those who abide by the world's standards.

> *"If you were of the world, the world would love its own; but because you are not of the world, but I choose out of the world, therefore the world hates you."*

> *"Blessed are you when people revile you and persecute you and utter all kinds of evil agains you falsely on my account."*

Anger, resentment, bitterness; show ostentation; power, conflict, hatred ring out like a noisy gong, a clanging cymbal; the harsh sound of metal against metal; the hammer against the nail — disrupting, bleeding, destroying human relationships. But the power that heals, that reconciles, that blesses us is more like the silence of eternity, interpreted by love.

THE NAIL
OF CRUELTY

The Nail Of Cruelty

Lent 5

Surely he has borne our
infirmities
and carried our diseases;
yet we accounted him stricken,
struck down by God, and
afflicted.
But he was wounded for our
transgressions,
crushed for our iniquities;
upon him was the punishment
that made us whole,
and by his bruises we are
healed.

— Isaiah 53:4-5

I don't know of any time in my life when I have sought more anxiously a relief from the intensity of the drama of the Lenten season. I know that it is not time yet, that the suffering and agony of the crucifixion must precede the joyous proclamation of the resurrection. Yet my heart and my mind revolt against this continual confession of personal inadequacy, of personal pride and guilt. Never before have I longed so for the peace and comfort which my church can give me; for the contented and comfortable feeling which the gospel can proclaim, that all is according to God's plan and the taste of victory and the vision of glory are already upon us. Yet I know that it is not time yet; for in my impatience I am met with the awesome patience of God, who traveled the road of suffering, persecution and death before revealing himself in the new life of the resurrection.

These nails are beginning to hurt; I no longer wish to hear nor preach about the nail of pride, the nail of hatred, the nail of envy, the nail of indecision, the nail of infidelity, the nail of cruelty. I am ready . . . ready . . . ready for the comic relief from this tragic drama. I am tired of being told and of telling how guilty I am . . . we are. I want to comfort and be comforted. I want to tell funny stories and make people laugh . . . as I laugh with them.

But God's entry into history was more than a colorful drama. It was a flesh and blood person. Christianity is more than a story whose ending we can change or manipulate for our own purposes. It is a life shared with Christ, which means sharing his crucifixion as well as his resurrection.

The rhythm of the church year shows me this. It reflects the rhythm of life and faith. Life, as well as faith, is not a stable state, but a rhythm, an alternation, a succession of new births. It does not go on indefinitely in an unchanging pattern, but springs up anew from generation to generation, from birth to birth.

The message of resurrection and victory would mean nothing if we knew nothing of the battle over which the victory was claimed. The message of liberation would mean nothing if we did not recognize the shackles that keep us sub-human.

And so, once again, we come to contemplate that which we would rather ignore . . . the nail of cruelty.

> *Surely he has borne our*
> *infirmities*
> *and carried our diseases;*
> *yet we accounted him stricken,*
> *struck down by God, and*
> *afflicted.*
> *But he was wounded for our*
> *transgressions,*
> *crushed for our iniquities;*
> *upon him was the punishment*
> *that made us whole,*
> *and with his bruises we are*
> *healed.*
> — Isaiah 53:4-5

Where do we find the nail of cruelty in all this? Surely we would not be among those who actually inflicted physical punishment upon Jesus. None of us here tonight is of the type who would actually crucify a person in the flesh. Few of us would take to the dagger or pistol to bring revenge upon the object of our hatred.

But there were others besides the soldiers around the cross that day. Mark tells of those who mocked him, saluting with derision: "Hail, King of the Jews." And there were those who "passed by deriding him, wagging their heads saying, 'Aha! You who would destroy the temple and build it in three days, save yourself, and come down from the cross.' " The chief priests made fun of him, saying, "He saved others; he cannot save himself." And those who were crucified with him also reviled him.

This is our Lord: one who was reviled, mocked and laughed at. A suffering servant, who though he was in the form of God did not count equality with God a thing to be grasped, but

53

emptied himself, humbled himself and became obedient unto death, even death on a cross.

Certainly this is a fitting climax for one who claims to submit to ultimate suffering, that he should be rejected by the very ones for whom he suffered.

What we see in this man Jesus is a paradigm of what it means for us to be fully human. It sets before us a human life of concern and love that includes suffering, death and resurrection victory.

The suffering and death are not ends in themselves; rather they are an embodiment of the ultimate reality of all life. This is the shape of God's presence among us; it is the form that God's dwelling among us takes — suffering, death and victory.

Jesus' love was an actual living with and for others. It is a law of existence that if you love someone long enough and deeply enough, that love will entail suffering. A casual love, a superficial concern, can avoid suffering, because it backs off when the going gets rough. The deep sort of concern and sharing that characterized Jesus' love persists until the end, even to suffering and death.

And it is of this love, suffering and death that Paul writes: Through him God chose to reconcile the whole universe to himself, making peace through the shedding of his blood, upon the cross; to reconcile all things; whether on earth or in heaven, through him alone.

I am not altogether sure that we can accept such a doctrine of atonement. I am not altogether certain that we are big enough to accept it. If we make any attempt to affirm such a belief in atonement, it will stagger many of the cherished notions that we have held about ourselves, both as individuals and as a Christian community.

Can we accept an understanding of atonement that insists upon reconciliation with all persons? This is a stern test indeed of our life together in this place. Can a community that has built into its very essence the idea of being an elite group really accept the assertion that it is subhuman except it be reconciled with the rest of society, the non-elite segments of humankind.

Can a group of people that is in nearly every sense privileged both financially and intellectually, beyond the dream of most of our society, really identify its destiny, its very humanity, with the less privileged? Or must we always look upon those other segments of society as lazy, unfortunate, or unnecessary? I suspect that very few of us include their destinies as an integral part of our own. But unless we see their humanity as a part of our own, we do not take Christian atonement seriously, nor Christian humanity seriously. To take these seriously means to willingly and joyfully participate in the Christian mission of suffering love.

If alienation, not reconciliation, is at the center of your life, becoming involved is the antidote . . . "rejoicing with those who rejoice and weeping with those who weep" . . . but always so that hope does not get swallowed up by love, so that prayer does not vanish in the white heat of action or become a brisk recital to pep us up and improve our action.

As Evraf says in *Doctor Zhivago,* "Remember, you must never, under any circumstances, ultimately despair. To hope and to act, these are our duties and misfortunes. To do nothing and finally to despair is to neglect our duty."

Why is it both our duty and misfortune to act? It seems to be a cruel consequence of human existence that to act is to invite a risk, a chance. An illusion to the realm of law clarifies this. Suppose you are standing by while a small baby is crawling toward an open well. You decide to try to save the baby before he falls into the well, but in your attempt to grab him at the edge, you inadvertently push him over the edge. According to the law you are guilty of misfeasance. But suppose you merely stood by and watched the baby crawl to the edge of the well and fall in. Your inaction would then be described as non-feasance for which you are in no way guilty under the law.

Jesus was never a passive bystander, a "non-feaser." He showed what it meant to be fully human, to take the real risk of living.

To live the Christian life is to take the risk of acting, becoming involved, opening the doors to outsiders, not closing yourself off in safety behind your walls and barriers.

To hope and to act, these are our duties and misfortunes. To do nothing and finally to despair is to neglect our duty.

Yes, it would be easy for most of us to non-fease our way through life — to do nothing and finally despair. But Christ asks us to follow a different way: to take the risk of living. He took it. It cost him the nail of cruelty, but he took it. Yet cruelty and death did not hold Jesus. Christ did not vanish, but rather he showed that blind alleys could be opened up to be paths to life, frustrations could be cleared away. Life could be cleared away. Life could be found where before people could except only destruction.

This is what it means to say "Jesus is Lord." Those are the most glorious words you shall ever hear. Cling to them, repeat them for yourself, make them your own and you will come to realize that the nail of cruelty was one of the nails that shed Christ's blood up on the cross, so that you might be reconciled to God and to one another. For in being reconciled to God, you will find yourself reconciled with others.

The Banner

This series deals with ways we continue to divide and punish one another and the body of Christ through our sins.

One option to enhance worship during Lent is to create a banner for use in the worship area. The banner has two options. First, all the nails may be added when the banner is originally created and hung. Second, the banner may be created and one new nail may be added each week. You will find that attaching Velcro to the nails helps in the weekly updating of the banner.

The suggested dimensions of the banner is 44-inches by 36-inches. You may chose any colors you wish. We suggest a purple background, white letters and grey nails. The scale on the grid is one square equals four inches.

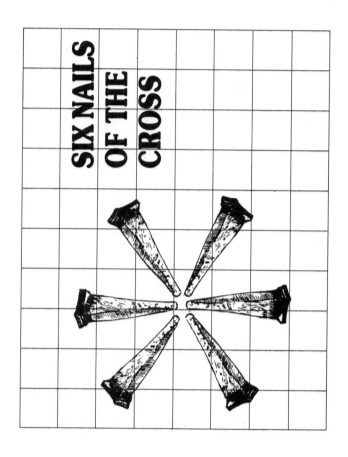

Scale: 1 square = 4 inches